Housekeeping with DOROTHY WORDSWORTH at Dove Cottage

by
Margaret and Robert Cochrane

With drawings by
Trevor Galvin

Highgate of Beverley

Highgate Publications (Beverley) Limited
2001

Acknowledgements

The authors wish to thank the following: John Markham for his patience and advice; Trevor Galvin for his illustrations; Jeff Chowton and his staff at the Wordsworth Archive; Alan Humphries, Librarian, the Thackray Medical Museum, Leeds; the staff of the Armitt Library, Ambleside and R. Twining and Co. Ltd, of Andover, Tea and Coffee Merchants.

Abbreviations used in Notes

WW William Wordsworth
DW Dorothy Wordsworth
RW Richard Wordsworth
STC Samuel Taylor Coleridge
JM Jane Marshall
EG Elizabeth Gaskell
MH Mary Hutchinson

British Library Cataloguing in Publication Data.
A catalogue record for this book is available from the British Library.

© 2001 Margaret and Robert Cochrane

Margaret and Robert Cochrane assert the moral right to be identified as the authors of this work.

ISBN 1 902645 23 5

Published by

Highgate of Beverley

Highgate Publications (Beverley) Limited
4 Newbegin, Beverley, HU17 8EG. Telephone (01482) 886017

Produced by Highgate Print Limited
4 Newbegin, Beverley, HU17 8EG. Telephone (01482) 886017

Contents

List of illustrations	iii
Acknowledgements	ii
Abbreviations used in notes	ii
1 A Dream Comes True	1
2 Food and Drink	7
3 Housekeeping	17
4 Some Occasions	23
5 Charity	27
6 Outdoor pursuits	29
7 Reading and Writing	35
8 Caring for Children – and William	37
9 Dorothy Through the Eyes of Others	41
10 The End of a Dream	42
Appendix I	45
Appendix II	45
Notes on text	47
A Select Bibliography	48

List of Illustrations

Title page: Silhouette of Dorothy Wordsworth
Courtesy of the Wordsworth Trust

Drawings:
- Page 2 — Townend: Dove Cottage as it was
- Page 11 — The Kitchen
- Page 20 — The Sitting Room
- Page 24 — Gallow Hill
- Page 32 — Grasmere
- Page 39 — The Houseplace

Cover Photographs:
Front: The Houseplace
Courtesy of the Wordsworth Trust

Back: Dove Cottage as it is today
R. E. Cochrane

My youthful wishes all fulfilled –
Wishes matured by thoughtful choice.
I stood an inmate of this vale,
How could I but rejoice?

From *A Winter's Ramble in
Grasmere Vale*
by Dorothy Wordsworth

1

A Dream comes True

On a cold winter's day in 1799 as dusk was spreading across the waters of Grasmere, a post-chaise drew up outside a cottage facing the lake. A small woman alighted, accompanied by a tall thin man. The glow of the fire through the window reflected the glow in Dorothy Wordsworth's heart as she contemplated making the first real home she and her brother William would share together.

Dorothy, born at Cockermouth in 1771, was a year and a half younger than her famous brother, William. She had three other brothers, Richard, John and Christopher, of whom she was very fond, but it was William that she idolised. Apart from being close in age William and Dorothy were close in temperament, being sensitive, observant and sometimes melancholy. When she was only six years old she was sent to stay at Penrith with her grandparents while her mother paid visits to the south. Unfortunately, Mrs. Wordsworth contracted consumption and, on her death, her wish was for Dorothy to be sent to live with her cousin's family, the Threlkelds.

Dorothy arrived at the comfortable Threlkeld home on a typical June day in 1783. Only seven years old, she was small in stature, nervous in manner and now an orphan. Her mother had made a wise choice of guardian. Elizabeth Threlkeld was ideal; an intelligent cultured woman, used to children. Related by marriage to the Wordsworths, she lived in Halifax, where her husband was a pastor. When Dorothy was ten years old she spent six months at boarding school in Hipperholme, and from the age of thirteen attended a day school where she made many friends; the foremost of these was Jane Pollard, the eldest daughter of a prosperous mill owner. Jane eventually married John Marshall, a manufacturer from Leeds. She and Dorothy corresponded for the rest of their lives and much of the knowledge of Dorothy's early life is to be found in their letters. The happiness Dorothy found in Halifax, however, could not compensate for the parting with her brothers. After ten years, her grandparents requested that she return to them. At sixteen she was lonely and miserable in their home and all she could look forward to was the return of her brothers from school. She longed for a home of her own which she could share with William, he writing, and she housekeeping and was happy when they were offered the loan of a furnished house at Racedown in Dorsetshire. They lived there for two years and, during this time, formed their friendship with Samuel Taylor Coleridge. They were then lucky to be able to rent cheaply a large furnished house, Alfoxden, near the Quantock Hills in Somerset, not far from Coleridge's house. After a year, they decided to go on an extended tour of Germany, where they thought the living would be cheaper, returning to England in early summer, 1799, staying with their friends, the Hutchinsons at Sockburn–on-Tees.

While at Sockburn, William, his brother John, and Coleridge, went on a walking tour of the Lake District. William was entranced by Rydal and Grasmere and wrote to Dorothy of a plan to build a house by the side of the lake. Later he saw a small empty house which might be suitable for them. He decided to drop the idea of building, which, with the state of their finances at that time, was probably something of a pipe dream, and take the empty cottage. In the same letter he told Dorothy she had been left a legacy of £100 by her uncle Crackenthorpe and suggested this could be spent on furnishing and domestic items for the house.

In previous years the house had been an Inn, the Dove and Olive Bough, leading to the name Dove Cottage. The front windows looked straight over the road to Grasmere. Behind were a garden and an orchard, quite small and rising steeply. A typical Lake District seventeenth-century cottage, it was the fulfilment of

Townend: Dove Cottage, as it was.

2

Dorothy's childhood dream. William and Dorothy left Sockburn on 17 December. George Hutchinson accompanied them on horseback as far as Wensley, having lent William a horse and carrying Dorothy behind him, and then returned home with the horses. From Wensley, the brother and sister walked over the tops to Kendal, some fifty to sixty miles. Here they bought furniture and household requirements and completed their journey by chaise, arriving at Dove Cottage on Friday, 20 December 1799 at 4.30 in the afternoon.

It was dark and cold, but a neighbour, old Molly Fisher, had come in and lit a fire every day for a fortnight ready to welcome them. In later years she remembered Dorothy standing by the hearth in a striped gown and straw bonnet warming herself. As usual when moving into a new home the first few days were chaotic. Both Dorothy and William caught colds, one of the chimneys smoked badly, walls needed painting, carpentry jobs needed doing, bed curtains were to be sewn and hung and, to make matters worse, Dorothy developed toothache. In spite of it all they were both pleased – this was their home, their furniture, and would be their way of life.

The house was entered through a narrow front door into a house-place or kitchen hall, measuring sixteen feet by twelve feet. The ceiling was low and beamed, the walls panelled with dark stained wood. Beneath the diamond-paned window was a window seat; the floor was of slate. There was a fireplace at one end of the room where Dorothy later did some cooking. Opening out of the house-place was a small room which they decided to use as a bedroom. Dorothy slept here for some time. Behind this was a kitchen with a larder which had a stone slab and a spring running under the floor. On the first floor were two rooms facing the front. The one over the house place they decided would be their sitting room where William could write and they could entertain friends. Next to it was the room which became William's bedroom. A small room above the kitchen was at first used as a lumber-room, and a tiny room, no bigger than a cupboard, opened off it. The earth closet was in the garden at the back of the cottage. A visit there entailed a trip through the front door and all the way round the house – not a pleasant prospect in a howling gale or snowstorm. Later, to shorten the journey, another door was cut through the cottage wall. With the rising land this had to be halfway up the stairs to the upper floor but led straight out into the garden – a great improvement. It was William's job in snowy weather to clear the path to the privy, but that was a minor problem when the distance was so much shorter than it had been. Over the time Dorothy and William lived there further alterations were made to accommodate the changes in their circumstances but, for now, this was perfection. It was to be their home for the next nine years.

Dorothy made it her business to get to know the neighbours. Old Molly Fisher, her brother and his wife, lived just across the road. Although money was short Dorothy decided to employ her to help with the rough work for two hours a day, and extra time to help with laundry and visitors. Her wage was to be two shillings (10p) per week plus her dinner. 'We could', wrote William to Coleridge, 'have had this attendance for eighteen pence, but we added sixpence for the sake of the poor woman who is made happy by it.'[1] Molly was sixty years of age and Dorothy wrote to Jane Marshall that 'she was very ignorant, very foolish, and very difficult to teach, so that I almost despaired of her.'[2] She, nevertheless, was devoted and honest and proud of her job. Thomas Ashburner with his wife and five children was another near neighbour. Dorothy soon discovered he had been what is known in the Lake District as a 'states-man' – a freeholder with a small plot of land farmed by himself and his family. He had been unable to make the farm pay and had been forced to sell up. He made a living selling coal from Keswick and doing various odd jobs. Dorothy bought her coal from him and sometimes he helped them in the Dove Cottage garden. Another useful acquaintance was John Fletcher, the carrier. He rented a peat-house next door to Ashburners in which to keep his horses and carts. He was often employed by the Wordsworths to carry letters and packages. Not far away lived the Lewthwaite and Dawson families, some of whose members later worked for Dorothy. These, of course, were all 'working class' people whom Dorothy described as, 'excellent people, friendly in performing all offices of kindness and humanity, and attentive to us without servility . . .'[3] She continues in the same letter to Jane Marshall: 'We are also on very intimate terms with one family of the middle rank of life, a clergyman with a very small income, his wife, son, and daughter.' This was the Simpson family. Reverend Joseph Simpson,[4] a sprightly eighty-year-old, often went fishing with the Wordsworths, and Dorothy described his wife as a 'delightful old woman, mild and gentle in her manners, and much of the gentlewoman'.[5] The daughter was pleasant and their son interesting. They were close friends and useful to each other as they were some distance from the shops. Very few days passed without the families meeting to take tea, play cards or help each other out by lending and borrowing various household items.

However Dorothy's most intimate friend in the district was Catherine Clarkson, wife of Thomas, the well-known campaigner for the abolition of slavery. The Clarksons lived at Eusemere on Ullswater but had to leave in 1803 for the sake of Catherine's health. The letters exchanged between her and Dorothy give us much information about life in Dove Cottage. The support of neighbours and friends was essential to Dorothy's housekeeping. Although at this time they had little money, they lived well – the barter system was a great help. When one family had a surplus of crops grown in their garden they would give it away or exchange it with someone else. In this way everyone benefited from the regular gluts of vegetables, plants, flowers and dairy produce.

There was no strict timetable to life at the cottage. There was time to walk, to write, to row on the lake, as well as for Dorothy to perform her household tasks. Time was theirs to use as they pleased. To quote Dorothy's words, 'our employments are not very various, yet they are irregular',[6] She was happier than she had ever been.

Even the time of rising varied greatly. Breakfast was eaten in the upstairs sitting room, where Dorothy could boil a kettle on the fire, as the kitchen fire was not lit until later. It may seem strange to modern taste but William took broth for his breakfast with a plate of bread and butter. To fit in with whatever they were doing, dinnertime was whenever they chose. Dinner was eaten in the kitchen parlour any time after ten o'clock. Their menu was very varied: it included all the meats, game and poultry, freshwater fish, seasonal vegetables and fruits. Dorothy, a thrifty cook, made pies with leftover meat or giblets for the next meal. She wrote one time: 'Baking bread, apple pies and giblet pie – a bad giblet pie – it was a most beautiful morning.'[7]

Tea was taken, like dinner, when convenient and, if the weather were fine, they would sit lingering over it in the orchard. Often friends and neighbours joined them and stayed on to gossip and play cards; on one occasion in October 1802 there were 13 of their neighbours in to tea. They did not buy their tea locally as at that time it was often adulterated with the leaves of trees such as hawthorn and beech, or even sheep droppings. They usually bought it from Richard Twining, a reputable London tea merchant and an old friend of their uncle, William Cookson. Sometimes brother John would send them a box of tea. Dorothy dried the used tealeaves and gave them away to her poorer neighbours.

The quality and amount of supper varied according to what

meals had been eaten during the day and who was in the cottage at the time. If Dorothy were on her own she would eat quite sparingly just one dish such as hasty pudding, tapioca, broth or a boiled egg. If Coleridge were visiting, the food was more lavish: mutton chops and potatoes, hare or something equally tasty. William sometimes enjoyed cold mutton or broiled sausages. After the dishes were washed it was the custom to let the kitchen fire out to save fuel. It was not lit again until it was time to cook the dinner the next day. Molly, the servant, slept at home so there was no need to keep the kitchen heated – just another of Dorothy's economies.

Of course, the original idyll of peace and solitude could not last. In late January 1800, John, the Wordsworths' younger seafaring brother, arrived. He was very shy and quiet, not having seen Dorothy for almost seven years. He was so nervous that twice he turned back from the door and eventually went to the inn and sent a message that he had come. He proved to be the perfect guest, fitting in comfortably with his brother and sister, helping them put the finishing touches to the cottage and turning his hand to many of the more practical tasks around the house and garden. In early spring, while John was still at Dove Cottage, Mary Hutchinson came for a six-week visit. The Hutchinsons were old family friends from the days when Dorothy had lived in Penrith with her grandparents. Mary had attended the same dame school as William and had become friendly with Dorothy.

Before Mary left, Coleridge arrived to stay for a month. He wanted to inspect a house, Greta Hall, being built at Keswick, with a view to moving there with his family and to be near the Wordsworths. He gave no consideration to the fact that he was uprooting his wife and children from their friends and family in the South and moving them 300 miles to the North, to live in what was to all intents and purposes a jerry-built horror. It was what he wanted. Throughout their friendship and his frequent visits to the Wordsworths his attitude was selfish and thoughtless but in spite of this he was a loved and welcome visitor. Much later, Mrs. Gaskell, describing a dinner with Mary Wordsworth wrote: 'It is curious, the loving reverence she retains for Coleridge, in spite of his rousing the house about one in the morning, after her confinement, when quiet was particularly enjoined, to ask for eggs and bacon! and similar vagaries.'[8]

After William's marriage to Mary Hutchinson and the subsequent births of their children, Dove Cottage was bursting at the seams. Mary and Dorothy shared the housekeeping, nursing and childminding, most of the work often falling to Dorothy. Not until the family left Dove Cottage in 1808 did her role change, and then not very much. She lived with William and Mary for the rest of her life, sharing with the forbearing Mary her love for her brother and his family.

2
Food and Drink

Much of Dorothy's day was taken up with baking and cooking. The following is quoted from her journal for August 1800: '– boiled gooseberries – N.B. 2lbs sugar in the first panfull [*sic*] 3 quarts all good measure – 3 lbs in the 2nd 4 quarts – 2½ lbs in the 3rd – a very fine day.' Possibly more of a preserve than boiled fruit. The following recipes are of her time and use only ingredients mentioned in her journal or letters. For the sake of modern cooks a conversion table of weights and measures is given in appendix i. Oven temperatures and timings are modern. Dorothy would have had to judge the temperature of the oven from her own experience. Skill was also required in managing the fire both for cooking in the oven and on the open hearth. Thank goodness we do not have the vagaries of cooking with Dorothy's equipment.

Breakfast

William's Hearty Broth – serves 4
    1½ lb shin beef or neck of mutton
    Salt and pepper
    1 carrot, peeled and chopped
    ½ turnip   do   do
    1 large onion, skinned and diced
    2 leeks, cleaned trimmed and thinly sliced
    3 potatoes, peeled and diced
Method
    Remove the fat from the meat and cut into bite sized pieces. Put the meat in a saucepan and cover with 4 pints of water. Add seasoning. Bring to the boil, cover and simmer 1½ hrs. Add the vegetables, re-cover and simmer further until the vegetables are soft. Skim off any fat that has formed on the surface with a spoon or a piece of kitchen roll. Taste and adjust seasoning as necessary. Serve very hot, garnished with a little chopped parsley.
    The Wordsworths ate it accompanied by bread and butter.

Dinner

Herby Pork Chops – serves 4

    4 pork loin chops   1 egg beaten
    2 oz fresh breadcrumbs   salt and pepper
    1 tablespoon chopped fresh parsley
    1 teaspoon chopped fresh mint
    ½ teaspoon chopped fresh thyme

Method

De-rind chops and place in a single layer in a baking tin. Mix remaining ingredients and spread evenly over the chops, pressing it down slightly. Bake in the oven at 200ºC/400ºF/Gas mark 6, for 45-50 minutes. Serve hot.

Gammon with Scalloped Potatoes – serves 4

    1 lb peeled sliced potatoes
    1 slice raw gammon ½ inch thick
    1½ cups of milk
    1 tablespoon chopped onion
    a little made mustard

Method

Brown gammon on both sides in a frying pan. Place it on a fireproof dish and spread with the mustard. Cover with the chopped onion and sliced potatoes and add the milk. Cover the dish and bake in a slow oven 150ºC/300ºF/Gas mark 2 for 1 hour. Uncover and bake for further ½ hour.

Grasmere Poached Pike

    A 3-4 lb pike   salt and pepper
    4 pts court bouillon

Method

To make the court bouillon use 4 pints of water with a little vinegar added. Combine with vegetables such as celery, carrot and onion. Add a bouquet garni of parsley thyme and bay leaf. Simmer for 30 minutes and allow to cool.

Place pike in a fish kettle and pour over the court bouillon, cover and poach for 40 minutes over a gentle heat with the lid on. When cooked drain the fish. Serve garnished with parsley, accompanied by melted butter.

A contemporary recipe for fish seasoning

    ½ oz white pepper   ½ oz nutmeg
    ½ oz mace   ¼ oz cayenne

Grind together

Cheesy Apple Pie – serves 6

For the pastry
8 oz plain flour   4 oz Wensleydale cheese, crumbled
4 oz butter
For the filling
1 lb cooking apples, peeled cored and sliced
2 oz dried fruit   2 oz Wensleydale cheese, crumbled
A good teaspoonful of clear honey
Beaten egg or milk to glaze

Method

Pastry – sift flour into a bowl, rub in the butter. Add crumbled cheese. Add enough cold water to make a dough. Roll out half the pastry and line an 8" pie dish. Mix the apples, sultanas, honey and cheese and fill the pie. Make a lid from the remaining pastry, cutting a small hole in the top to let out the steam. Use any spare pastry trimmings to decorate the top of the pie with leaf shapes. Brush with milk or beaten egg and bake at 200ºC/400ºF/Gas mark 6 for 20-30 minutes.

Apples were one of William Wordsworth's favourite fruits. He enjoyed them raw, baked, in pies, tarts and dumplings. While William was away, Dorothy wrote in her journal for 8 March 1802: 'here is one of his bitten apples! I can hardly find it in my heart to throw it into the fire.' The cool larder, with the spring running under the floor, made an ideal apple and vegetable store.

Baked Apples

4 large baking apples   2 oz (¼ cup) sugar
¼ teaspoon ground cinnamon   2 oz (4 tablespoons) butter
⅓ pint apple-juice or cider   8 teaspoons rum

Method

Core the apples, leaving a small piece at the bottom end to prevent the filling running out. With a sharp knife cut a hairline circle round the apples to prevent them bursting. Arrange the apples in a round baking dish. Fill the cores with sugar and add a teaspoonful of rum. Dust with cinnamon and place a knob of butter on the top of each apple. Pour the apple-juice/cider into the bottom of the baking dish. Cook at 180ºC/325ºF/Gas mark 3 for 45 minutes, or until tender, basting the apples with the liquid from time to time

When cooked remove from the oven. Pour into each apple a second teaspoonful of rum and baste with liquid. Stand for 5 minutes as they will be very hot. Baste again and serve with cream.

A Fruit and Batter Pudding
    4 oz plain flour   1 egg beaten
    2 oz sugar   1 oz butter
    Pinch of salt   ½ pint milk
    4 tablespoons of fruit, e.g. gooseberries, plums
Method

Mix flour with salt and sugar. Add the beaten egg, a little of the milk and mix well. Gradually beat in the rest of the milk until a smooth batter is obtained. Place butter in baking tin and place on top shelf of the oven at 200ºC/400ºF/Gas mark 5. When smoking hot, pour in the batter and add the fruit. Bake for about 30-35 minutes till well-risen and golden brown. Serve with single cream.

Batter puddings were sometimes cooked by boiling without the addition of fruit. Small puddings could be made this way by using less ingredients and putting the batter in a teacup tied with a cloth and boiled in a pan of water.

Teatime

Cake baking at this time was more difficult than it is now because baking powder and self-raising flour had not been invented. It was necessary to use a different raising agent. Yeast was available but this was not suitable for every purpose. The deficiency was remedied by using more eggs, the yolks and the whites being beaten separately. William was very fond of parkin and gingerbread. In a joint letter to Coleridge – they were obviously sending him supplies – William tells him: 'Dorothy is packing up a few small loaves of our American flour, as to the pepper-cake[9] which I promised, it died of a very common malady, bad advice. "The oven must be hot, perfectly hot." said Molly the experienced, so into a piping hot oven it went, and came out (but I hate the antitheses, in colours especially) black as a genuine child of the coal hole. In plain English it is not a sendable article.'[10]

The next two recipes are from a hand-written notebook from the early 19th century. Although the ingredients are shown, no instructions are given. Make of them what you will!

You will note that the recipe for pepper-cake states 'cook in a slow oven.' Probably Molly's exhortations that the oven must be

The Kitchen, Dove Cottage

'hot, perfectly hot.' were the cause of the burnt offering.

Pepper-cake
    3 lb flour   ¼ lb butter
    3 lb treacle   ½ lb candied lemon peel
    ½ oz ground ginger   ½ oz Jamaica pepper
    ½ oz coriander seeds   ¼ oz black pepper
    1 oz best Jerusalem currants 1 cup of water
Cook in a slow oven.

Parkin
    2 lb treacle   ½ lb butter
    ½ lb soft sugar   2 oz ground ginger
    1 handful of flour
    and as much sifted oatmeal as to make a stiff paste
Cook in a slow oven.

The very last entry in Dorothy's Journal, Sunday, 16 January, 1803 describes how she bought gingerbread from blind Matthew Newton who had lost his sight many years previously in a quarry accident and was now an itinerant bread merchant. She writes: '– intensely cold. William had a fancy for some gingerbread. I put on Molly's cloak and my spenser[11] [*sic*], and we walked to Matthew Newton's – I went into the house – the blind man and his wife and sister were sitting by the fire, all dressed in their Sunday's Clothes [*sic*], the sister reading. They took their little stock of gingerbread out of the cupboard and I bought 6 pennyworth. They were so grateful when I paid them for it that I could not find it in my heart to tell them we were going to make gingerbread ourselves. I had asked them if they had no thick. "No" answered Matthew "there was none on Friday but I will endeavour to get some." The next day the woman came just when we were baking & we bought a pennyworth.' Dorothy baked seed cake for old Mr. Simpson, the sprightly parson. Caraway seed was very much in vogue at the time and seed cake was often eaten as part of a funeral feast. The following recipe from *Mistress Margaret Dods Cook and Housewife's Manual* published in 1829 shows the use of beaten eggs. It is hardly suitable for a modern cook!

A Fine Seed Cake

Take a pound and a half of flour, and 16 eggs, well whisked. Mix with a pound and a half of fine beat sugar, and whisk them well together. Throw in a half pound of cut candied citrus, lemon and orange peel, and four ounces of almonds blanched and cut. Mix this with a pound and a half of dry flour and twelve ounces of butter beat to a cream [*sic*]. Season with cinnamon, cloves and throw in a few caraway seeds. Smooth the top of this (and every sort of cake) when put into the hoop and throw sugared caraways over it.

It is unlikely the one Dorothy made for Mr. Simpson would have been as complicated as that but the principle would have been the same.

Pies and Pastry

Pies figured quite largely in the diet at Dove Cottage. Pastry was much easier to make than cakes and could either be sweet or savoury. Tarts made a variation on the theme. Favourite pies were curd, apple, gooseberry and rhubarb; savoury, veal and giblet. Pies were economical and convenient, easily divided into portions if unexpected visitors arrived, and they were filling.

There are many varieties of pastry, but a basic recipe would be:

    ½ lb flour   4 oz lard
    ½ teaspoon salt   water

Sieve the salt and the flour into a basin. Chop the fat into small pieces and rub them into the flour with the tips of the fingers until the mixture becomes crumbly. Add water, gradually mixing it in until a stiff paste is formed. Take out and knead very gently. Roll out and use as required. This can be enriched by using more fat, substituting butter for lard, or half-and-half butter and lard, or by sweetening or adding the yolk of an egg according to taste.

Gooseberry Tart

    1½ pints of gooseberries
    ¼ lb short crust pastry
    ¼ lb moist sugar

With a pair of scissors top and the tail the gooseberries. Put them in a deep pie dish, pile the fruit high in the centre and put in the sugar; line the edge of the dish with short crust, put on the cover, and ornament the edges of the tart. Bake in a good oven for about ¾ hour and before serving dredge with castor sugar. (Delicious served with cream).

Supper

Hasty Pudding – a very old recipe – no quantities given.

    milk   sugar   flour
    sago or tapioca   salt

Method

    Boil up the milk. With the left hand sprinkle in sufficient flour, sago or tapioca, stirring briskly meanwhile. Add a little salt and sugar to taste, stir, and cook for about ten minutes. Serve with cream, jam or treacle.

Tapioca Pudding

    1 pint milk   2 tablespoons of tapioca
    1 tablespoonful sugar 2 eggs
    nutmeg   salt

Method

    Boil the milk, sprinkle in the tapioca, stir until boiling and simmer until it becomes clear, stirring occasionally. Add the sugar and a good pinch of salt, and, when a little cool, the eggs beaten. Pour into a greased pie dish and bake in a slow oven for about ½ hour.

    Here is another recipe from Mistress Margaret Dods, this time for
Lamb Chops with Potatoes, which she describes as 'a favourite dish.'

Cut the back ribs of a large lamb into handsome chops, trimming off the bone with a chopping knife. Season, and brush the chops with a beat egg; dip them in crumbs and minced parsley and fry. Nicely place mashed potatoes (made somewhat thin with butter and cream and again heated) high in the centre of the dish. Score this neatly and lay the hot chops around, leaning each chop on the side of the adjoining one. A finely minced onion may be added to the mashed potatoes if the flavour is liked.

Bread
Although the staple food of the ordinary people in the Lake District would be oatcakes – oats were easier to grow than wheat in wetter areas – Dorothy does not mention them in her *Grasmere Journals*. In his *Guide to the Lakes*, William talks of eating oaten cake, new and crisp, at a shepherd's house in Martindale. There is evidence in her *Recollections of a Tour in Scotland, A.D. 1803* that she did make them. As usual, Dorothy displayed a great interest in the ways of the people where they stayed. At one house where they lodged overnight she recalls: 'I went to talk to the mistress who was making Barley cakes, which she wrought out with her hand as thin as the oaten bread we make in Cumberland. I asked her why she did not use a rolling-pin, and if it would not be much more convenient, to which she returned me no distinct answer, and seemed to give little attention to the question: she did not know, or that was what they were used to, or something of that sort. It was a tedious process and I thought I could scarcely have managed if the cakes had been as large as ours; but they were considerably smaller, which is a great loss of time in baking.'

There are many recipes for oatcakes, varying according to the part of the country in which they were made. There are two basic types: the first being made from a stiff paste, rolled out with a rolling pin and baked on a griddle called a bakstone. This was sometimes known as haverbread or havercake, (haver came from the Old Norse '*hafri*' meaning oats: cf haversack – originally a bag for food) or clapbread or clapcake if flattened by hand. The second was made from a batter containing yeast and baked by pouring or throwing it on the bakstone; this type was called either riddlebread or oatcake. It was obviously the first type Dorothy was familiar with.

Oatcakes
  8 oz fine oatmeal   ½ level teaspoonful of salt
  1 oz butter   pinch of bi-carbonate of soda
  cold water to mix

Method

Place the oatmeal, salt and bicarbonate of soda in a bowl. Rub in the butter and add enough cold water to mix into a firm dough. Knead lightly on a surface dusted with oatmeal until the dough is smooth. Cut out into round biscuits and place on a greased tray. Bake for 1 hour at 150ºC/300ºF, gas mark 2. Allow to cool.

Dorothy's Grasmere journals do, however, frequently refer to baking bread. In those days flour contained all the wheat germ that is now removed from white flour. Dorothy's bread would have resembled the modern wholemeal loaf. Yeast was not always easily obtainable and so it was 'grown' from a small quantity of good yeast to provide enough for the large quantity of bread made. The yeast Dorothy obtained from Mrs. Olliff would be the starter and she would have used one of several methods to grow it. The 'receipt' [*sic*][12] she passed on to Charles Lloyd and Mr Simpson was probably for this process.

Wholemeal Bread makes 4 1lb loaves

    3 lb wholemeal flour   2 oz fresh yeast
    1 level tablespoon sugar   3 level teaspoons salt
    1½ pints warm water (not hot)

Method

Mix salt and flour. Mix the yeast with the sugar in a little of the warm water and leave for about ten minutes to froth, then add to the flour. Add the rest of the water and mix well by hand for several minutes until the dough leaves the sides of the bowl clean. Turn onto a floured board and knead for ten minutes. Put in a bowl in a warm place to rise, covered with a cloth until it has doubled in size, then return to floured board and knead again until firm. Divide into four and flatten each piece to knock out air bubbles. Place in greased 1lb loaf tins and leave in a warm place to rise again for 1 hour.

Bake for about 30 minutes at 230ºC/450ºF/Gas mark 8 until bread shrinks from side of tins and loaves are browned. Remove from tins and place on a wire rack to cool. If the loaves sound hollow when tapped on the bottom they are cooked.

The wheat grown in England used to be 'soft' wheat as opposed to the 'hard' wheat grown in warmer climes. Hard wheat could be ground finer and made better and whiter bread. In a letter[13] Dorothy referred to making little loaves using the 'best flour from America'. This barrel of flour was a very welcome gift from Robert

Griffith, a cousin of Dorothy's mother. He had befriended her during her miserable stay at her grandparents' home. He went to America, where he married, and became a prosperous shipping merchant. The flour would only be used for best baking as it was so superior to the more coarse kind used every day.

Beverages and Alcohol

The Wordsworths were great tea drinkers. As mentioned previously, they bought their tea (and coffee) from Richard Twining, a member of the tea firm founded in 1706, to ensure it was fresh and unadulterated. They usually purchased a large amount about once a year. Twinings sent it from London, by carrier, to Mr Thomas Cookson, merchant of Kendal, and, after the canal system was extended as far as Kendal, it was sent by barge using Pickfords. Tea was expensive, costing around seven shillings a lb, and they used about 20lb per year at Dove Cottage. Later on, 25 October 1828, Dorothy ordered from Twinings the prodigious amount of 75lb Souchong, 30lb Congou, (both black teas) and 6lb good West India coffee (roasted). As they moved up in the world, so did their consumption of tea.

It is surprising that the firm of Twinings has managed to survive through the years with customers as slow paying as the Wordsworths. This was due to the dilatoriness of their brother, Richard, who was supposed to look after their financial affairs. Dorothy wrote to him in July 1809 asking him to pay Twinings £13. 14s. for tea purchased the previous September and saying she had ordered a further supply.[14] A month later she wrote again hoping Twinings had been paid as she had now received the new order.[15] In January 1810 she wrote asking him to pay £31. 16s. for tea supplied in August 1809, part of which was for Mr Cookson, the merchant in Kendal, who had already paid her for his share of the order.[16] Obviously Richard took little notice as in May she was again writing[17] to say she had received a bill from Mr Twining for £29.12s for the September, 1808 and the August 1809 orders plus £13.18s for the tea ordered for Mr Cookson, 'altogether £45.10s'. Her arithmetic seems at fault in this letter, although the total agrees with amounts mentioned previously. This is equivalent to around £4,500 in today's money. A considerable sum for two years' tea!

Far from being the 'simple water drinking bard' described in his poem, *The Waggoner*, William, and also Dorothy, enjoyed something a little stronger. In common with most families Dorothy brewed ordinary ale for the household, but they were more than delighted when Sir George Beaumont sent them a cask of a superior brew, which they pronounced excellent.

During her many bouts of sickness Dorothy found drinking wine a help. At Christmas 1802 she wrote to Richard:[18] 'I am quite recovered from my late illness and I hope to continue in good health by taking scrupulous care of myself. I continue to drink wine though not in so large quantity as I did. I find myself stronger and better for it, but I hope in summer I shall be able to leave it off again.' However, the next year she was explaining to Richard[19] that she needed to draw upon the funds for £5 extra as she had been 'obliged to drink wine' – an expensive habit.

Rum seemed to have been very popular. At one time they had acquired a cask of rum and had to borrow bottles from the Simpsons. Mr Simpson also enjoyed his tot, calling in at Dove Cottage at bedtime when he was passing on his way home. Warm rum and water was a comforting nightcap on chilly evenings, but the elderly Mr Simpson still had two miles to go. On one occasion, when Dorothy called on the Simpsons to take tea, both he and his son were 'tipsy', and another time his son called at Dove Cottage again 'tipsy'. Perhaps this was why Dorothy went to them for bottles.

Brandy and water fortified Dorothy on one of her walks with William and Coleridge, 'I drank a little brandy and water and was in heaven.'[20] Water was available from a well in the garden that William with the help of John Fisher had cleaned out. When walking they would drink from the streams.

3

Housekeeping

Laundry

One of the most time-consuming household tasks was dealing with the washing. Without the aid of electricity, modern appliances, detergents and synthetic fabrics, it could take several days. Much depended on the weather – rainy wash days were things to dread. Drying clothes round the fire meant a damp steamy atmosphere all over the house. If the weather was cold, it also meant that one could not get near enough to feel the warmth of the fire and windows and cold surfaces would be streaming with condensation.

Dorothy and Molly had a weekly wash when small items, such as towels, waistcoats, stockings and petticoats which did not need a lot of ironing, were laundered. Then about every 5 weeks came the 'great' wash when larger things were included. The Wordsworths were lucky in that they had a 'place apart from the house' where this could be done.[21] The 'great wash' created a large amount of work, beginning with the heating of the water. The actual washing of the clothes, hard work though it was, was only part of the process. Rinsing involved carrying buckets of clean water to the tub which had to be emptied between washing and rinsing. The clothes had then to be wrung out and, where appropriate, starched. The starch granules were dissolved in cold water and then boiling water added to make a translucent mixture. If the weather was fine clothes were hung out in the garden to dry and the linen spread on bushes to bleach in the sun. After drying, came the ironing, mostly done by Molly though Dorothy sometimes helped. Apart from starching items to stiffen them, the starch when ironed created a glaze, which helped items such as curtains to keep clean longer. The whole business could take up to four days.

After William's marriage to Mary Hutchinson and the arrival of children, to say nothing of the constant stream of visitors, the house was teeming and the amount of washing increased. The 'great wash' became too difficult for Molly to manage, even with Dorothy's help, so Dorothy hired a woman to come in every five weeks for two or three days to help with the extra work.

Sewing and mending

Whenever Dorothy had a spare moment to sit down she would take up her sewing. She made, altered and mended their clothes. For the house she made mattresses, curtains and bed hangings. As they had little money to spend on clothes, and new clothes were costly, they mostly wore second-hand. Brother Richard sent his cast-offs to William. These were carefully repaired and altered. She unstitched Richard's coats but sent these to a tailor to be refitted; William had to be well turned out at all costs. Sara Hutchinson sent boxes of shoes and gloves and waistcoats, again, more sewing for Dorothy, who made new waistcoats and spent many hours mending stockings.

For herself she made shifts and petticoats and altered and mended dresses. Repairs to her white gown took a whole morning. Around the house Dorothy wore 'shoes' which she made for herself. These were really light felt slippers, which many women wore at that time. Sometimes she would sit and sew beside William while he worked at his poetry or read to her – an idyllic picture of cottage life. However, in June 1803 she let herself go. She wrote to Richard that, in expectation of the settlement of money due from Lord Lowther, she had spent nearly £20 buying clothes, something she had never done before.[22] Most of the money went on petticoats and shifts – a change from 'going from year to year with a scanty supply'.

Not only did she sew for herself and William, and later his children; she also made frocks for Coleridge's children and wristbands for his wife. She even found time to help other people, quilting a petticoat for an acquaintance, Aggy Fleming. For the cottage, in addition to making valances, bed hangings and curtains, she also repaired and bound carpets, which must have been very hard on the fingers. She bought sacking in Ambleside for the mattresses which she sewed with a packing needle. True to her principles, nothing was wasted. She kept any pieces of usable material in rag boxes which she often tidied and looked through to see if she could find a use for any of them.

Painting and Decorating

In June 1803 Dorothy wrote to Catherine Clarkson: 'will you get for us two pounds of green verditer the same as Betty Ritson got for us, also the proper quantity for Ivory Black for making the black.' Redecorating was not just a question of a visit to the nearest D.I.Y. store or calling in the professional. Paint had to be ground, often at home, as Dorothy described in her journal entry for Thursday, June 24 1802, and the coloured pigments bought in from specialist suppliers. The verditer referred to is a pigment made from copper nitrate, which produces a green colour. It could also produce blue by adding caustic lime. The ivory black was made from calcined ivory. When decorating was necessary, Miss Simpson came in to help – she coloured the walls while Dorothy whitewashed the ceiling. William helped for a short while but housework was not his forte. It was best left to the women. After Molly left her employment at the cottage to be her brother's housekeeper, Dorothy was without domestic help for six weeks. She and Mary carried out the Whitsuntide Spring clean, including

Sitting Room, Dove Cottage.

painting and colouring. Mary was not strong and most of the work fell upon Dorothy who declared herself to be 'overwrought with positive labour'.[23] A new servant was due to start and she wanted everything in order. Not all the rooms were painted. Dorothy papered William's room herself the second year they were in the cottage, and papered the small cupboard-like room upstairs with newspapers, an economical and effective alternative that also provided additional insulation. The ever-generous Sir George Beaumont, a keen amateur artist, gave them two pictures. One, Dorothy's favourite, was of Applethwaite Dell. This was the land Sir George had given to William. It hung in a place of honour above the chimneypiece; the other, Conway Castle, hung in Dorothy's bedroom where she studied it while she was dressing. There are several references in the Grasmere Journal to Dorothy gathering mosses. She used them to decorate the chimney piece but they probably dried out quite quickly. Sometimes she used ivy and wild berries for the same purpose. She very rarely picked wild flowers – she either transplanted them into the cottage garden or left them alone. She made their home comfortable and welcoming by her efforts.

Health and Home Remedies

In common with many people at the time, Dorothy had very bad teeth and was a prey to toothache all her life. When the pain became too great she took laudanum to alleviate it. This was easily obtainable in various patent medicines which could be bought at any grocer's shop. A popular local brand was 'Kendal Blackdrop'. When one day a tooth broke, she wrote in her Journal: 'My tooth broke today. They will soon be gone. Let that pass I shall be beloved – I want no more.' Her health was never robust and she frequently complained of headaches, which were often bad enough to force her to go to bed. She had frequent bowel and stomach problems – phrases like, 'I had a woeful headache and was ill in my stomach' and, 'I was ill in my bowels' – are often found. She took castor oil and considered asking Coleridge to send her some bark and castor oil. She described her symptoms to Catherine Clarkson in the hope that Catherine would try to learn from her own physician, Dr. Beddoes, what could be done to cure them. 'I began with sickness, violent headache, yellow and pale looks, and afterwards came on [obscured]ness with pains in the bowels, thirst, and want of appetite – I then had no sickness but what seemed to come from weakness and pain', and later in the same letter, 'By the bye if it seems to be worthwhile, you may tell Dr. Beddoes that at all times when I am not in uncommon strength (as I was before the last attack) after writing for any length of time or doing anything that exercises my thoughts or feelings, I have a very uneasy sense of want and weakness at my stomach, a mixture of emptiness, gnawing, and a sort of preparation for sickness – eating always removes it for a time.'[24] She tried drinking wine.[25] Dr. Beddoes sent Dorothy a prescription and advice concerning diet which she followed. On the other hand, she wrote of William to Sara Hutchinson, 'Really it is almost a pleasure to be ill, he is so good and loving to me.' When Molly had a sore toe she again turned to Catherine: 'Old Molly has a very sore toe to which I wish very much to apply your famous medicine. Pray by the first opportunity send us a bit that she may try it.'[26]

William too enjoyed ill health! He suffered from piles and chronic indigestion for which he dosed himself with a 'stomachic' medicine. A contemporary treatment for piles was as follows:

2 oz lard, 1 drachm camphor, 2 oz powdered gall [sic] and ¼ oz laudanum. The resultant ointment was to be applied every night at bedtime. A simpler remedy was honey and lard mixed together. (These recipes are printed for interest only and <u>should not be tried.</u>) He also had continuing problems with sore eyes and took to wearing a green eye-shade. Leeches were used as a treatment for fever and choleric temperaments. The children were vaccinated against smallpox. Edward Jenner had recently popularised this treatment and the Wordsworths obviously believed in keeping up with the latest medical advances.

Accidents in the kitchen were as common then as they are now. When Dorothy scalded her foot with hot coffee she almost fainted and had a bowel attack. Applications of vinegar were applied and she went to bed. On another occasion she burned herself with Coleridge's Aqua Fortis (nitric acid). She does not explain what Coleridge used it for, but at that time it was believed to have medicinal properties. It was used (presumably suitably diluted) as an antiseptic and also taken internally as a tonic and for a variety of serious diseases, including typhoid, hepatitis and syphilis. At full strength it could be heated and the fumes used as a fumigant in rooms where there had been cases of contagious diseases.

Small burns or wounds were treated by sewing on a bandage (a strip of material) to hold a pad with ointment over the wound. A doctor would only be consulted in the most serious circumstances.

Finances

The Wordsworths' financial arrangements were, to say the least, not straightforward. Their father, John, had been a lawyer in the service of the Lowther family, Bailiff and Recorder of the Borough of Cockermouth and Coroner of the Seignory of Millom. After his death, it was found that most of the funds he left were in the hands of Sir James Lowther. Sir James, Lord Lonsdale, was a mean and dictatorial man and he refused to release to the family their due.

Their brother, Richard was also a lawyer. He was practising in London and doing well, so the family delegated to him the task of trying to obtain what was rightfully theirs. He was also in charge of the little money there was, paying out their meagre allowances and attending to their legal correspondence. He was not always as quick and efficient as the rest of the family would have liked. Luckily for William, in 1795, just when his finances were at their worst, he was left £900 by his old school friend, Raisley Calvert, whom he had nursed in his last illness. The money was to be used to purchase one or more annuities and he was empowered to invest what portion he wished for the use of Dorothy. Richard was again to act for them.

At the time they moved into Dove Cottage, William's income was about £80 per annum. Fortunately, in 1799, Dorothy was left £100 by her uncle Crackenthorpe and used this to buy furniture for the Cottage. Although the rent was only £8 a year, it is easy to see why Dorothy needed to be a frugal and economical housekeeper. No wonder they wished the money Lord Lowther held to be released as soon as possible. In 1802, Sir James died. His heir determined to pay off the family debts, but it took Richard three years to sort out their inheritance. At last Dorothy would have some money of her own. Her share was £1,800 which was to have been used to provide her with an income for life, although some of it may have been invested in brother John's last fatal voyage. Thomas De Quincey wrote that most of her fortune perished with his ship: 'How much I never felt myself entitled to ask; but certainly a part of it was on that occasion lost irretrievably.'[27]

In 1803, Sir George Beaumont gave William a farmstead at Applethwaite, at the foot of Skiddaw. It consisted of a few old cottages and two small fields valued at £100. The Wordsworths' finances were now eased and they could afford some luxuries in their diet, such as more butter, wine and potted fish, a local delicacy. They also bought slates to mend the roof. For himself William purchased new gloves and a hat, but Dorothy's frugality was ingrained and she still spent very little on herself.

4
Some Occasions

William's Marriage

On Monday, 4 October 1802, William married Mary Hutchinson at All Saints Church, Brompton, halfway between Pickering and

Scarborough. It was a strange occasion. Mary's brothers, Thomas and John, and her sister, Joanna, were witnesses. William was described on the Marriage Certificate as 'gentleman'. No member of his family attended. The ceremony in the church was quick and quiet. Although Dorothy had accompanied William to Mary's home at Gallow Hill, she did not go to the church. In view of Dorothy's feelings for William, it was a very traumatic and emotional time. She knew that following his marriage to Mary she would no longer be mistress of Dove Cottage, but she also knew she was to continue to live there and would not be parted from William. She understood the necessity for him to have a wife and family but now the time had come found difficulty facing it. She just wished it was all over and she was back home.

The night before the wedding ceremony, William had given her his wedding ring to wear and, when she took it off in the morning, he slipped it on to her finger again and blessed her. As word came from the church that the proceedings were over, she could 'stand it no longer' and threw herself on her bed. There she stayed until Mary's sister, Sara, who was preparing the

Gallow Hill.

wedding breakfast, came and roused her when the wedding party was coming up the avenue. She ran out to meet them, flinging herself into William's arms, and he and John Hutchinson escorted her back to the house, Mary following behind. After the breakfast was over, William, Mary and Dorothy began their journey by chaise back to Grasmere. There was no honeymoon.

Christenings

Nine months after their wedding, William and Mary's first child, John, was born. On 17 July 1803 Mary was churched, a special service to give thanks for a safe delivery, and John was christened. Dorothy stood as godmother and Coleridge and Richard Wordsworth as godfathers. Richard was unable to come so old Mr Simpson stood proxy for him. In the afternoon a party was held and they enjoyed christening cake, tea and coffee while the baby slept in his basket – a meat basket which had cost half-a-crown.

The following year the Wordsworths' second child, Dorothy, was born three weeks early and was christened a month later. Lady Beaumont was invited to be godmother and Sara Hutchinson stood proxy for her. Shortly afterwards Lady Beaumont sent £10 as a christening gift. It was decided to spend the money planting with trees a small plot of land to be called Dorothy's Grove.

In June 1806 a third child, another boy, was born. There were many discussions and doubts as to his name. At first he was to be called William but, after their problems with having two Dorothys, they decided that to have two William Wordsworths in the house could cause confusion. Eventually they settled on Thomas. Mary had a very difficult delivery and was very weak and tired for some time afterwards. The christening was held when Thomas was a month and a day old. His uncle, Thomas Hutchinson, was his godfather and Mary Monkhouse, a cousin of the Hutchinsons, was godmother. This was the last of Wordsworth's children to be born at Dove Cottage.

A Pauper's Funeral

When a fifty-six-year-old woman was buried by the Parish, Dorothy, with about fourteen other people, attended the funeral. She noted that the black painted coffin was covered with a decent cloth and was neatly lettered. The cortège left from John Dawson's house near the Swan Inn and Dorothy was in tears while the mourners waited to set off. It was a beautiful sunny day and she thought the woman was going to a peaceful quiet spot. Unfortunately the priest, whom she had seen half drunk at the pot house the day before, was hardly in a fit state to take the service, which rather spoilt the solemnity of the occasion.

A Tea Party

When Molly's sister-in-law, Agnes Fisher died, Molly left her employment with the Wordsworths and moved back across the road to Sykeside and became her brother's housekeeper. It changed her life. She quickly put into practice all the household skills she had learned from Dorothy. She transformed the cottage from being the dirtiest house in Grasmere into a model of cleanliness and brightness. Her brother kept a cow and she made butter and cheese. Now she could meet Dorothy on a more equal footing, no longer as servant and mistress. Proud of her independence, she invited the Wordsworths to tea. This may not seem a very special occasion but to her and Dorothy it was a mark of her change in status. There was tea and coffee, piles of toast and as much cream porridge as little Johnny could eat. Molly was a proud and happy hostess and remained friendly with Dorothy for the rest of her life, often taking her small presents such as a bowl of curd, a pound of butter or a basinful of gooseberries. When she died she left her best gown as a legacy to Dorothy.

Christmas

Dorothy's birthday fell on Christmas Day. She wrote to Catherine Clarkson on 25 December 1805, 'Six Christmases [sic] we have spent at Grasmere, and though the freshness of life was passed away even when we came hither, I think these years have been the very happiest of my life.' She described how Johnny was highly excited at the thought of the two plum puddings boiling in the pot and the sirloin of beef roasting in front of the fire. Molly and John Fisher were invited to share in the feast.

It was the custom in Grasmere for the fiddler to visit houses in the area and half a dozen children from round about had gathered in Dove Cottage kitchen to dance. For days Johnny had looked forward to this but, when the occasion arrived, he was overcome with shyness and would only dance with his aunt. She danced with him until she was out of breath. She thought the sound of the children's feet pattering on the stone floor charming. It was a happy time and would long be remembered.

5
Charity

The first few years of the 19th century was a time of great poverty. Although there was a temporary lull in the fighting, the war with France and the blockade had upset trade and manufacturing. Wounded and old soldiers and sailors, widows, children, old people, and the unemployed were all driven to begging. The only help in alleviating it was Parish Relief but, to keep the poor rate down, each parish would only help those who could prove they belonged there. The majority received no help at all. Because of its location between Keswick and Kendal there were such hapless people walking the road seeking succour or employment. Dove Cottage was an ideal place for them to call. Dorothy took an interest in them, noting their appearance and their stories and recording them in her journal. She described them to William: the young widow carefully carrying a piece of paper she thought was a banknote; the little girl whose stepfather had turned her out; a young woman going to Kendal seeking work who was given a bed in a barn for the night.

Dorothy sometimes gave food instead of money. She gave bread to one woman and child who came to the door, noticing that the woman was exceptionally tall and that the child had bare feet. She gave hot tea to another poor woman and child, as they had had nothing warm on a cold November day. An old soldier, whose family were dead in Jamaica, received a piece of cold bacon and a penny. She could not help smiling when he called her 'a fine woman'. Once three beggars called in one day, the most surprising being 'a Merry African'[28] from Longtown. A sick-looking woman, with a thin pale little boy, came begging for rags to bandage her husband's leg. Dorothy was deeply affected and thankful that her life was not like that. She felt should be grateful for what she had. On another occasion a sailor came begging. He looked so like her brother John that she took pity on him at once; invited him in and sat talking with him by the kitchen fire for two hours. He said his name was Isaac Chapel and told hair-raising stories of his life at sea. One evening a hatter came begging. He had been ill for a long time and his wife was lying-in with their fourth child. They were unable to obtain Parish Relief because he was a tradesman who still had the tools of his trade and he was expected to go and find work. His plight obviously touched the Wordsworths for they gave him sixpence – a very generous sum at that time.

During their frequent walks they met many 'trampers' on the roads and Dorothy listened to their stories. A woman who said she had never begged before received a halfpenny and a crazy old man asked for a pin and a halfpenny. He went into Agnes Fisher's cottage and she gave him some whey and let him boil his porridge. Dorothy and William met a little boy who was begging for a measure of meal. He was about seven years old although he looked no more than five. When Dorothy asked him if he got enough to eat he looked surprised and answered, 'No,' as if he did not think anyone did. They met an old man bent almost double. A former soldier, he had been injured in a carting accident and was now trying to make a living gathering leeches. Dorothy recorded a detailed description in her journal and later William wrote *The Leech Gatherer* which was based on this meeting. A soldier carrying his child with his wife carrying his gun and a bundle were given some halfpence because 'it was such a pretty sight.' She was easily affected and gave a poor woman with two little girls a shilling, which she later realised was sixpence more than she should have done. A very old man who claimed to have been a servant of the Marquis of Granby told them his life story. Dorothy bought a pair of scissors from him. Although the Wordsworths were not rich they were generous and kind-hearted. While living at Racedown and Alfoxden before coming to Grasmere the Wordsworths employed a servant, Peggy Marsh. When Dorothy heard that her house had burnt down she asked her brother, Richard, to send her £2 on their behalf. When Sir George Beaumont learned of Peggy's disaster he sent her £5.

In 1806 tragedy hit the village. George and Sarah Green, parents of Sally the fourteen-year-old hired to help with the Wordsworths children, had gone over from Easedale, above Grasmere, to a sale. On their return journey the weather closed in, with mist and heavy snow. They lost their way and perished in the cold. At home they had left their six children, all younger than Sally, one a babe in arms. When their parents did not return, the children supposed they had stayed in Grasmere on account of the blizzard. They stayed in all the next day waiting for them to return and on the day following one of the boys went to a neighbour's house to borrow a cloak for his sister. When asked why he wanted it the boy explained that she was going to look for their parents. Immediately the neighbour realised what might have happened and raised the alarm. Fifty or sixty men left their work and began searching the fells. The women folk, including Mary and Dorothy, went to the cottage and were horrified to find the poverty there: hardly any food in the house, no money, and much of the furniture had been sold. Arrangements were made for the immediate care of the children. It was two more days before the bodies were found.

Normally the parish looked after orphans by boarding them out in the village. The standard of care varied and some were badly treated. Because of the tragedy in this case a subscription fund was set up to augment the parish resources. William and Dorothy wrote to their well-to-do friends and, largely as a result of their efforts, the sum of £500 was raised. This enabled the children to be well educated, placed in good positions and able to earn their own living when they grew up.

The Wordsworths themselves fostered Sally. Not as a servant, but to be sent to Grasmere School and educated as the others were. She would also be taught to sew. Although she was not very bright, and would never make a good maid, she proved adept at needlework. In view of this and, as there was still money available in the fund, the Wordsworths arranged for her to be apprenticed to a mantua maker.[29]

6
Outdoor Pursuits

Gardening

The garden at Dove Cottage was Dorothy's delight. Loving nature as she did, it was a constant source of physical and spiritual pleasure. She never regarded gardening as a chore but as an act of creation. For the heaviest work she could recruit William or John Fisher and Molly helped with the weeding as a change from working indoors. As soon as they arrived in the cottage Dorothy began to plan what she wanted from the garden. William too had definite ideas about gardening, and indeed later planned and laid out a winter garden for Lady Beaumont at Coleorton, near Ashby de la Zouche. Brother and sister agreed that nature should harmonise with buildings, each complementing the other.

On first seeing the garden, William writes to Coleridge, Dorothy, in her imagination, 'has already built a seat with a summer shed on the highest platform of this, our little domestic slip of mountain. The spot commands a view, over the roof of our house, of the lake, Helm Cragg, and two thirds of the vale.' Although the garden and orchard were both overgrown this was no deterrent. As soon as the weather was suitable they went into action. They pulled down the existing wall at the front of the garden and moved the boundary two or three yards further forward to separate them more from the road and to provide room for flowers. A fence dividing the orchard from the garden was removed.

Brother John came to stay at Dove Cottage shortly after their arrival, helping with the digging and tree planting. The whitewashed walls of the cottage were thought to be too stark so Dorothy fixed threads over them and grew runner beans, roses and honeysuckle up them. Not only did the scarlet flowers of the beans look attractive but also they were a prolific source of food. Vegetables were an essential part of the diet, so many varieties were grown. She grew herbs in pots that she kept in a recess on the sunny south side of the cottage.[30]

The countryside round about provided Dorothy with many plants native to the area and she set to with a will collecting and transplanting them. She gathered and saved seeds from flowers, such as her favourite white foxglove, and obtained new plants from blind Matthew Newton. Wordsworth planted boxwood round the house and a yew tree at the front. He and John Fisher cleaned out the well and built up a short curved terrace walk high up the sloping ground. Below this was a small pool planted round with primroses and approached by a stone stairway. In 1802 William and Dorothy made a kind of bower or 'Indian shed' there so that they had somewhere to sit on warm days.

During her tour of Scotland in 1803 Dorothy noticed what was called in the local dialect a 'fog house' – fog meaning moss. She wrote: 'On the outside it resembled some of the huts in the prints belonging to Captain Cook's voyages, and within was like a haystack scooped out. It was circular, with a dome-like roof, a seat all round fixed to the wall, and a table in the middle – seat, wall, roof and table, all covered in moss in the neatest manner possible. It was as snug as a bird's nest; I wish we had such a one at the top of our orchard, only a great deal smaller.' In 1805 her desire became reality when a moss-hut was built in the orchard, towards the northern end of the top wall and very much a version of the fog house. It proved a boon to the family – warm to sit in in winter and cool in summer. They used it as an extension to the house, holding tea parties in it, writing there in peace or just relaxing and admiring the view.

On one of his many visits to Dove Cottage Coleridge discovered a rock seat in the orchard. It was covered with brambles and thistles that Dorothy helped him clear away. He was so tired by his efforts he took to his bed after tea – but not so tired that he could not eat the broiled mutton chop which Dorothy served to him in bed!

Dorothy received help and plants from friends and neighbours. To help the garden flourish she gratefully accepted the offer of a load of manure from John Olliff, a neighbour, but the malodorous task of spreading it fell to William. They kept bees in the garden and John Fisher planted sods round the bee stand to prevent the ground becoming too muddy. Thomas Hutchinson gave her two shrubs to plant.

As the Wordsworth children arrived and grew they enjoyed playing in the garden with their friends from neighbouring cottages. Writing to Sir George Beaumont, William describes the idyllic scene: 'I write to you from the moss hut at the top of my orchard, the sun just sinking behind the hills in front of the entrance and his light falling on the green moss of the side opposite me. A linnet is singing in the tree above, and the children of some of our neighbours, who have today been little John's visitors, are playing below, equally noisy and happy; the green fields in the level area of the vale and part of the lake lie before me in quietness.'[31]

Any time was a good time for Dorothy to be gardening. She describes planting lemon thyme by moonlight, sowing spinach and kidney beans on a cold evening, nailing up trees in the wind and transplanting honeysuckle in the rain. When Mary Hutchinson arrived as a bride at the Cottage she was immediately taken to see the garden by candlelight, so anxious was Dorothy to introduce the garden to her that she could not wait for daylight.

When the family left Dove Cottage Thomas De Quincey took over the tenancy. To Dorothy's horror and dismay he cut down the hedge round the orchard and every bush that screened it. He had the ash tree pollarded, destroyed the moss hut and levelled the ground. Dorothy was so hurt and angry that she said she would never speak to him again.

A list of plants grown by Dorothy is given in appendix ii.

The Lake

It is not surprising that the lake, being so near, played a large part in the Wordsworths' leisure activities. It was also a source of free nutritious food and helped to eke out the housekeeping money. At first they borrowed a boat from William Gell, a friend who lived on the other side of the lake from Dove Cottage. Sometimes they made up fishing parties, on one occasion catching 13 bass, but more often went on their own. They obtained from Robert Newton pike floats which they baited with small fish and set in the lake, went trolling, which entailed trailing a long line with baited hooks behind the boat, and sometimes fished from the bank with rod and line. At other times they fished for trout, which could also be caught in the many streams.

 The little boat was used for excursions to the island in the middle of Grasmere, where they had picnics, and for visits to other favourite spots around the lake. Dorothy describes how she, William and Coleridge sailed down to Loughrigg, letting the boat

Grasmere.

take its own course, while they read poetry. In hot weather William, though not Dorothy bathed in the clear water.

In winter, if the frost was hard enough, the lake became an ice rink. In letters to Lady Beaumont and to Catherine Clarkson, Dorothy describes how William and George Hutchinson, on skates, had pushed her and Mary, seated on chairs with the children on their knees, over the ice. She describes it as 'one of the most delightful days that ever was'. William wrote of his memories of skating in Book One of his autobiographical poem, *The Prelude*. His skates are still in existence.

Walking

It is well known that William Wordsworth enjoyed walking, but so did Dorothy. She often accompanied him on his walks but also walked alone or with Coleridge or Mary. If the walk was to be of a long distance, they took food such as cold pork and mutton, sandwiches of potted beef, or bread and cheese. Occasionally they would call at a farmhouse to buy milk or bread. Dorothy records walking to Keswick on a clear frosty morning in November 1800. She set off at five minutes past ten in the morning and arrived at half past two in the afternoon, having covered a distance of 13 ½ miles in four and a half hours – brisk walking by anybody's standard. She sometimes broke her journey when she walked the same way, stopping at John Stanley's inn, the Kings Head at Thirlspot, for tea or ale and bread.

In their ramblings the Wordsworths made the area even more their own by naming woods, rocks and hills and William wrote *Poems on the Naming of Places*. When they first arrived at Grasmere they named Easdale The Black Quarter. A wood at the north-east end of Grasmere Lake became Brothers Wood. A stand of fir trees almost opposite the wood became John's Grove. After John drowned when his ship the Earl of Abergavenny sank in 1805 they often came here to think of him. Named after Mary Hutchinson, a rock in Bainrigg Wood became Mary Point, and a rise in the ground was named after Sara, who also had a rock named after her. The initials of William, Dorothy, John Wordsworth and Mary and Sara Hutchinson were all carved into it. In the 1890s, after the reservoir at Thirlmere was made, it was necessary to build a new road. The Rock of Names, as it had come to be known, obstructed the work and was blasted away by the navvies. Attempts were made to cement the pieces together and they are now to be seen, fixed into natural slate and embodied into a rock face behind the Wordsworth Museum.

Dorothy's favourite walk was on White Moss Common, named after the abundant cotton grass which grew there. The place seemed to her to have magical qualities, 'a place made for all kinds of beautiful works of art and nature, woods and valleys, fairy valleys and fairy tarns, miniature mountains, alps above alps'. Dorothy suffered from headaches and sometimes walked for the fresh air and exercise to alleviate the pain. She was not deterred by the weather, walking in rain, hail and snow, fierce wind or burning sun and became quite weather-beaten. Her slight short figure stooping forward as she walked was a well-known sight.

Travel

Although by nature unsophisticated, Dorothy was no stranger to travel. Before coming to Grasmere she and William had lived for a year in Germany mostly at Goslar. In his early twenties William had visited France and had had a liaison with Annette Vallon with whom he had a daughter. In 1802, The Treaty of Amiens had made it possible to go to France and, Dorothy and William decided that, before his marriage to Mary Hutchinson, they would visit Annette and see his nine-year-old daughter, Caroline, for the first time. They travelled to London and on to Dover. William wrote his famous poem, *Composed upon Westminster Bridge*, while riding on the top of the Dover coach. Strangely, Dorothy records very little of this time although they were there for a month. On their return she was seasick all the way across the Channel and was greatly relieved to arrive in Dover.

The next day was very hot and she and William bathed and sat on the Dover cliffs from where they could see the French coast. On their return to London they spent a few days lodging near Charles and Mary Lamb, who were delighted to see them. Charles took them to Bartholomew Fair, a colourful and boisterous experience. On the way back they diverted to Gallow Hill, North Yorkshire, where William married Mary Hutchinson a few days later. They returned to Grasmere and Dorothy was pleased to be home.

Shortly after the birth of William's first son, Wordsworth, Dorothy and Coleridge set off for a six-week tour of Scotland. Although it did not include the far north, they covered a lot of ground. It was a great adventure getting as far as Glencoe and Loch Tummel. They travelled in their 'outlandish Hibernian vehicle'[32] – their Irish cart drawn by a nervous horse – taking with them necessities such as tin cups, umbrellas, cushions, cloaks and greatcoats. The practical Dorothy included ground coffee, tea and sugar. The roads were bad, the weather often wet and gloomy, the cart broke several times, the accommodation was usually filthy, the food poor and the people sometimes unintelligible. Dorothy loved it. She wanted to know and feel. She did not come to criticise but to observe. She noted with lively interest the sights, sounds and smells. Her prose pictures were equal to many in William's verses, albeit more homely, not so grandiose, and the more human for that. Coleridge did not like it one bit. He could not stand the noise of the cartwheels; he hated sitting in the rain and cold and was thoroughly miserable. After two weeks, he had had enough roughing it and left them to return home. The brother and sister pressed on with their journey, Dorothy looking out for cottages where they might obtain food and lodging for the night.

They met Walter Scott and his wife and immediately liked them. When they returned home they began a correspondence that lasted for years. Dorothy later conveyed her impression of Scott to Lady Beaumont: 'He is a man of very sweet manners, mild, cordial and cheerful.'[33] The tour had been a success for the Wordsworths, if not for Coleridge. Dorothy wrote to brother Richard: 'You will be glad to hear that we are both much better for our tour into Scotland, we spent our time very pleasantly, saw a great deal, and returned in excellent health. To be sure it was rather expensive but what matter? We travelled as frugally as ever we could, and we shall have something pleasant to remember as long as we live.'[34]

7
Reading and writing

Dorothy had none of the usual social accomplishments required in a lady of the time, such as playing a musical instrument, painting or singing. She admitted to herself that her drawing was atrocious. Her attempt to sketch the shape of Dove Cottage in a letter to Lady Beaumont is proof, if proof were needed, of her lack of skill. She drew the front of the house but, when it came to perspective, it was entirely beyond her to draw the 'out jutting'.

She wrote: 'You may lament with me that I have not been taught to exercise a pencil. It is indeed true that I scarcely ever have a walk without lamenting it.'[35]

She did, however, enjoy reading and, at the age of 14, read *Clarissa Harlowe*, a very racy epistolary novel in eight volumes, by Samuel Richardson. Before she was 16 she had a small collection of books, including works by Shakespeare, Milton, Fielding and Goldsmith. The classics and foreign authors were not neglected. She had Homer's *Iliad* and *Odyssey*, *Gil Blas* by Lesage and copies of *The Spectator*. During their years at Dove Cottage her reading habit continued, with such books as Boswell's *Life of Johnson*, Spenser's *Mother Hubberds Tale,* and works by Chaucer. She and William often read to each other and sometimes, when he was sleepless, Dorothy would read him to sleep. To house the growing number of books they acquired, they put up book-cases, sent to them by Charles Lloyd, in a recess in the upstairs parlour. It was Dorothy's task to sort and file the newspapers she received and, when she had time, she kept up her study of German.

Dorothy spent much of her time making fair copies of William's work. Paper for 'best' work was bought at Pennington's in Kendal, a bookseller and printer's shop. For rough work she wrote to Richard and asked him to include in a box of cast-off clothes he was sending: 'Six quires of the largest size of writing paper for rough drafts: scribbling paper it's called in Cambridge.'[36] Dorothy herself used old notebooks to write her journal. Usually they made their own pens from quills. Mr Simpson sent them a parcel of quills which they would cut and point with William's pen-knife – when he had not taken it off somewhere. When he was going on a visit to Greta Hall they made pens to take with him and Dorothy was not pleased that he went off leaving her only two for her own use. Ink was very variable in quality, sometimes being watery, and, as can be seen from their letters, very susceptible to fading. Fortunately modern methods of conservation ensure they will last for many more years.

Dorothy herself made some attempts at writing poetry and William praised her efforts. She was too astute, however, not to realise he was biased in her favour and knew in her heart that her strength was prose. William had read two of her poems for children to Lady Beaumont, who wrote to her trying to persuade her to continue her efforts. She replied that she had made several attempts but had given up in despair. She declared: 'No one was ever so inept at moulding words into a regular metre.'[37]

8
Caring for Children – and William

It was fortunate for the Wordsworths that Dorothy possessed a strong maternal streak. While living at Racedown, before the Dove Cottage years, she had the opportunity to practise her child care skills. Basil Montague, a friend of William's, was a widower living in chambers in Lincoln's Inn with his three-year-old son, also named Basil. However hard he tried, it was obvious that he could not properly look after a child in these circumstances and he arranged with William, provided Dorothy agreed, for his son to be lodged with the Wordsworths and to pay William £50 a year for his board. Dorothy, fond of children as she had declared herself to be, had no objection, welcoming the little boy with motherly affection and forming the philosophy of child rearing that stood her in such good stead with her own nephews and nieces.

Modern parents could do well to study her loving yet sensible ideas. She wrote of her system to Jane Marshall: 'We teach him nothing at present but what he learns from the evidence of his senses. He has an insatiable curiosity, which we are always careful to satisfy to the best of our ability. It is directed to everything he sees . . . He knows his letters, but we have not attempted any further step in the path of book learning. Our grand study has been to make him happy.'[38]

When he first arrived he was spoilt, fractious and forever crying to get his own way. Dorothy's cure for this was to tell him that if he wanted to cry he could go into a certain room in the house, out of earshot, and get on with it. When he decided to stop he could come back. She would not deviate from this rule and soon Basil realised that she meant what she said. It worked out wonderfully well. She continued her letter: 'We have no punishments except such as appear to be, as far as we can determine, the immediate consequence that is to grow out of the offence.'[39] She had great pleasure and satisfaction in watching him develop naturally and healthily 'from a shivering half-starved plant into a lusty, blooming, fearless boy.'[40]

When her first nephew, Johnny, was born at Dove Cottage, she was in raptures. Mary only had a nurse for a few days and then Dorothy was left in charge. She wrote long letters to her friends, extolling the virtues of this wonderful child, so much so that William was afraid she would bore them witless: 'He has blue eyes, a fair complexion – a body as fat as a little pig, arms that are thickening and dimpling and bracelets at his wrists, a very prominent nose which will be like his father's and a head shaped upon the very same model. I send you a lock of his hair sewn to this letter.'[41]

Her letters describe him as he grows, the restless nights when he was teething, the need for a high chair, his childhood ailments and what sort of noise he made when he cried. She wrote letters with him sitting on her knee watching the movement of her pen. Looking after him seemed to agree with her – her health improved and she did not get as tired as she expected when she carried him out for walks. She loved to watch him as he learned to sit up by himself on the carpet with a work-basket full of oddments: 'he riots among it like a little pussy cat.' she wrote to Coleridge. Sometimes he toppled over and bumped his head but she knew he could not do any real damage and never made a fuss. In this way she thought he would soon learn to take care of himself.

Mary was glad of Dorothy's help as she became pregnant again quite quickly and, as Johnny was starting to walk, he needed constant watching. The new baby arrived, a month prematurely, on 6 August 1804. She was named Dorothy after her aunt but was called Dora to avoid confusion. Again she was received with delight, and Dorothy's pen was soon busy extolling the praises of her new niece. Johnny was very jealous and Dorothy had to watch him carefully as he often hit or pinched the baby to make her cry. Mary needed care too, as she was not as well as Dorothy would wish her to be. She was rewarded for her hard work by eventually seeing both Mary and Dora thrive.

When Dora was six months old, sad news of the Wordsworths' brother John arrived. He had been drowned with most of the crew when his ship, the *Earl of Abergavenny*, was wrecked. The family were distraught. Dorothy found some comfort in nursing Dora and found her quietness very soothing. In spite of her fragile nerves, she had also to cope, as best she could, with the boisterous Johnny. She would get up about seven in the morning to wash, dress and feed the children and then proceed with her household tasks while everything around reminded her of her brother.

Eventually she and Mary decided to divide the care of the children by each taking responsibility for them for half a day at a time. In that way both women got some time for other tasks, though really the only time the adults had a quiet period when they could talk together was when the children were in bed. Dorothy described the children's bedtime to Lady Beaumont: 'The hour before is generally a noisy one, often given up to boisterous efforts to amuse them, and the noise is heard in every corner of the house – then comes the washing and undressing, a work of misery, and ten minutes after, all is stillness and perfect rest. It is at all times a sweet hour to us . . .'

Busy as her life was, it was now to become even more so – Mary was again pregnant. Before the birth, Sara, Mary's sister, came to live at Dove Cottage and for the rest of her life made her home with the Wordsworths. Even without a new baby the cottage was now crammed – it would be impossible soon. William's second

The 'Houseplace, Dove Cottage

son, Thomas, was born on 15 June 1806. The birth was difficult and left Mary weak. Dorothy once more enthused to her friends over her new nephew. Like the other babies, Thomas slept in a basket, often when the women were busy in the kitchen, in a recess under the table where he could feel the warmth of the fire. He was the last of the Wordsworth children to be born at Dove Cottage, but, wherever they were born, Dorothy loved them all. She referred to them as 'our children' and was devoted to them. As she watched them at play, Johnny with his favourite Noah's Ark, Dora with her new doll, and little Thomas, she must have been pleased to be loved and needed by her family.

– And William

William Wordsworth suffered one of the worst problems that could affect a writer - he hated the physical act of writing, even to the extent that it made him feel ill. He would experience panic-attack type symptoms and came to loathe the sight of a pen, even to write a letter. Dorothy told Mary Hutchinson that he was always very ill when he tried to alter an old poem. In a letter to Coleridge, William wrote: 'Composition I find invariably pernicious to me, and even penmanship if continued for any length of time at one sitting.'

His handwriting was very poor and it became another of Dorothy's tasks to transcribe his work. This was no easy job as his poems were often written on odd pieces of paper, one stanza in one place and the next in another. Sometimes, if she could not spare enough time from her other duties, she would do this work at night after he was in bed. She also had the job of putting his work in order, arranging the pages, trimming them, making up covers and stitching them together. The many references in her Journal and letters about William injuring his health by writing show just how much she worried about him and just how much he relied on her help.

She wrote her own journal in various spare minutes through the day: sitting by the kitchen fire, in a quiet moment in the moss hut or even while William was eating his breakfast. She recorded many incidents and scenes which served to jog William's memory and which later found their way into his poetry. He himself said: 'She gave me eyes, she gave me ears.' She also gave him many hours of dedicated work.

9
Dorothy through the Eyes of Others

There is, unfortunately, no portrait of Dorothy Wordsworth except a very sad one painted in old age. Happily we do have word pictures of her, the impressions of friends and what she thought of herself. Coleridge's first recorded impression of her as a woman of 26 was written when she and William were staying with him at Nether Stowey: 'Wordsworth and his exquisite sister are with me – She is a woman indeed! – in mind I mean, and heart – for her person is such that if you expected to see a pretty woman, you would think her ordinary – if you expected to see an ordinary woman you would think her pretty! But her manners are simple, ardent, impressive. In every motion her most innocent soul beams out so brightly, that who saw would say, "guilt was a thing impossible in her". Her information various – her eye watchful in minutest observation of nature – and her taste a perfect electrometer. It bends, protrudes, and draws in, at subtlest beauties and most recondite faults.' When he came to know her better, he also noted that she lacked a sense of humour.

Ten years later, Thomas de Quincey gives us a description of his first meeting with Dorothy at Dove Cottage: 'Her face was of Egyptian Brown: rarely in a woman of English birth, had I seen a more determinate Gypsy Tan. Her eyes were not soft, as Mrs. Wordsworth's, nor were they fierce or bold; but they were wild and startling, and hurried in their motion. Her manner was warm and even ardent: her sensibility seemed constitutionally deep; some subtle fire of impassioned intellect apparently burned within her.' He noticed that she had an air of embarrassment and concluded by saying: 'I may sum up her character as a companion by saying she was the very wildest (in the sense of the most natural) person I have ever known; and also the truest, most inevitable, and at the same time the quickest and readiest with her sympathy with either joy or sorrow, with laughter or with tears, with the realities of life or the larger realities of poets.'

Her speech was quick and sometimes she stammered. Her movements were quick, impulsive and almost nervous. As she said of herself, 'It is natural in me to do everything as quick as I can, and at the same time.' She was a little over five feet in height with a slight figure, and when walking she stooped forward, which made her look rather ungainly. It was De Quincey who tells us that Dorothy was better known and more approachable than her brother. When people met the pair on their walks it was she they would speak to.

The poet Samuel Rogers and his sister met the Wordsworths on their Scottish tour in 1803. Although it was only a chance meeting on the road, many years later he had not forgotten the impression Dorothy made on him: ' She was a most delightful person, so full of talent, so simple minded, and so modest.'[42]

Unfortunately, as Dorothy lost her teeth, her appearance altered. Edward Ferguson[43] included in a letter to his brother in America a report of a visit by his sister, Mrs. William Threkeld, and her daughter, to Dove Cottage in the summer of 1805. They had not seen Dorothy for some time and were shocked by her looks. He wrote: 'Elizabeth gives a sad account of poor Dorothy, who is grown so thin and old that they should not have known her, lost many of her teeth, and her cheeks are quite sunk that it has entirely altered her profile.' She was only 34 years of age at that time, but she was content – she knew she was loved for herself not for her physical appearance.

10
The End of a Dream

By 1808, instead of a dream home for two, Dove Cottage had become an inconvenient and overcrowded home for seven, quite apart from the many visitors who came to stay. Sara Hutchinson, Mary's sister, had come to make her home with them and, in Dorothy's words, they were, 'crammed in our little nest edge full'.[44] Every bed had to be shared and camp beds used for guests. They were hoping that Coleridge and his son would come to them as he was determined to separate from his wife. Finding a new, larger home became imperative. That winter Lord and Lady Beaumont offered them the loan of a farmhouse at Coleorton on their Leicestershire estates. The thought of another winter in the overcrowded cottage was dreadful and they accepted gratefully. That Christmas, the Wordsworths, their four children, Sara Hutchinson, Coleridge and his son Hartley, a household of nine, were all living at Coleorton.

When they returned to Grasmere, although the Coleridges had left, it was still a tight squeeze and the search for a larger house continued. They eventually settled on Allan Bank, a large house above Grasmere, which they had condemned as an eyesore when it was being built. However, they now needed to find somewhere urgently, and the view looking out was much better than the view looking at it across the valley. As usual, the main burden of the removal work fell to Dorothy. Sara was too weak after an illness to be any help; Mary had sprained her arm and William 'was not expected to do anything'.[45] Fortunately, Mary's sailor brother, Henry, came to help. He was invaluable as he could turn his hand to anything. He also reminded Dorothy of her own dead brother, John. Although recently built, the house was found to be damp and uncomfortable with smoky chimneys and bad draughts. The rent was high and money was in short supply. Once again Dorothy was making curtains, binding carpets and stitching mattresses. At Allan Bank, another daughter, Catherine, was born to William and Mary – more work for Dorothy. In the larger house she had the comfort of having a room to herself but, even so, she missed Dove Cottage.

Coleridge and his son had come to live with them at Allan Bank but, following a bitter argument with William, he left the house and Dorothy was not to see him again for ten years. In 1810 Mary gave birth to her fifth child, a son, William, and Dorothy again took over the duties of nurse. They were on the move again the following year and arranged to rent the rectory opposite Grasmere Church. Although in summer it had seemed an idyllic spot, in winter the ground was boggy, the chimneys smoked just as badly as at Allan Bank and the outlook across the churchyard on a dull day was miserable. It was here in 1812 that little lame Catherine died, aged four. Six months later Thomas, who was six, died. Following these tragedies the family felt they could no longer live in the rectory or indeed in Grasmere – the memories were too painful. The search for another home began again. This time they arranged to rent Rydal Mount, quite an imposing house, a few miles from Grasmere, overlooking Rydal Water.

They moved on 1 May 1813 and spent the rest of their lives there. The household now consisted of William and Mary and their children, Johnny, Dorothy (Dora) and William junior together with Dorothy and Sara Hutchinson. This time Dorothy and Mary were able to buy new carpets, and extra furniture was bought at sales. Dorothy's circle of friends widened, the children were all at school and at last she had more time and privacy for herself and time for visits and visitors. She became interested in politics and William Wilberforce with his family stayed at Rydal

Mount for six weeks. A tour of the Continent was followed by a second expedition to Scotland. In London she visited the British Museum and all the latest exhibitions.

Sir Walter Scott visited them at Rydal with his son-in-law, who commented that Dorothy looked 'as yellow as a duck's foot'. In 1828 Dorothy, who was now nearing sixty was taken desperately ill with what was called 'internal inflammation'. She recovered, but was never really robust after that although she still found plenty to interest and absorb her. In 1831 she again became ill and these debilitating attacks continued until by 1834 her legs had lost their strength and she began to suffer from a form of arterio-sclerosis. In this distressing state she lingered on for another twenty years, faithfully attended by William, who would wheel her round the garden on fine days and soothe her in times of confusion.

When he was dying in 1850 she seemed to sense what was happening. Almost miraculously she managed to walk to his room to see him. After his death her condition worsened and she died in 1855 aged 84. Dorothy had spent her life in the service of William and knew she was loved. There was no other way she could have been happy. William acknowledged her love and devotion and her contribution to his final position as a great poet. In his words:

> 'She, in the midst of all, preserved me still
> A poet, made me seek beneath that name,
> And that alone, my office upon earth.'

Appendix i
Conversion chart for measures used in recipes

Weights
1 Ounce (oz)	25 Grams (g)
1˚ oz	40g
2 oz	50g
4 oz	110g
6 oz	175g
8 oz	225g
1 pound (lb)	450g

Volume
2 fluid Ounces (fl oz)	55 millilitres (ml)
˜ pint (pt)	150ml
1 pt	570ml
1˜ pt	725ml
1∫ pt	1,000ml = 1 litre (l)

These are all approximate conversions which have been either rounded up or down. Never mix metric and imperial measures in one recipe.

Appendix ii

List of plants grown in the garden as mentioned in Dorothy's writings.

A
Apple
Ash
Anemone nemorosa

B
Bachelors buttons (Rock ranunculus)
Barberries
Boxwood
Brambles
Broccoli
Brooms

C
Cabbages
Carrots
Celandine
Cherry tree
Columbine
Crab blossom

D
Daisies
Daffodils

F
Foxgloves
French beans

G
Geraniums
Gooseberries
Gowans
Grass
Greens

H
Heckberry blossom
Hepatica
Holly
Honeysuckle

I
Ivy

K
Kidney beans

L
Lemon thyme
Lettuces
Lilies (white and yellow)
London pride
Lychnis

M
Marsh marigold
Michaelmas daisies
Mulleins

O
Onions
Orchises

P
Pansies
Pear trees
Peas
Periwinkle
Pilewort
Plum trees
Potatoes

Primroses
Privet

R
Radish
Rhubarb
Roses
Rowan

S
Scarlet beans
Snowdrop
Sorrel
Speedwell
Spinach
Stitchwort
Sunflowers

T
Turnips

V
Vetches
Violets

W
Wild thyme
Winter cherry
Wood sorrel

Y
Yew tree

Dorothy's dearest wish, after moving into Dove Cottage, was to possess a book on botany, so she could look up the names of plants and flowers she found growing wild while on her walks. In 1801 William bought a copy of Withering's *An arrangement of British plants and an introduction to the study of Botany.*

Notes

1 WW to STC Dec 24 1799.
2 DW to JM 10.9.1800.
3 *Ibid*.
4 Sometimes referred to as Sympson.
5 DW to JM 10.9.1800.
6 *Ibid*.
7 Grasmere Journals 29.11.1801.
8 EG to John Forster 28.10.1852. *The Letters of Mrs. Gaskell*, Chapple and Pollard.
9 A kind of thick gingerbread.
10 WW &DW To STC 22.5.1801.
11 Spencer – a short waisted jacket.
12 Grasmere Journals 4.5.1801.
13 WW & DW to MH 29.4.1801.
14 DW to RW 22.7.1809.
15 DW to RW 20.8.1809.
16 DW to RW 9.1.1810.
17 DW to RW 9.5.1810.
18 DW to RW 25.12.1802.
19 DW to RW 15. 6.1803.
20 Journal 4.5.1803.
21 DW to JM 10 & 12.9.1800.
22 DW to RW 15.6.1803.
23 DW to Lady Beaumont 25.5.1804.
24 DW to C Clarkson 26/27.2.1804.
25 see Drinks and Beverages above.
26 DW to C Clarkson 7 or 14.6.1803.
27 Thomas de Quincey – *Recollections of the Lakes and the Lake Poets*.
28 Grasmere Journals 13.11.1800.
29 Dorothy Wordsworth, *George and Sarah Green, a narrative* (not published until 1936).
30 Prof. Knight, *Dove Cottage Grasmere from 1800 to 1900*. George Middleton, 1900.
31 WW to Sir George Beaumont 3.6.1805.
32 D. Wordsworth, *Recollections of a Tour in Scotland*. (1894).
33 DW to Lady Beaumont 4.5.1805.
34 DW to RW 16.10.1803.
35 DW to Lady Beaumont 26.8.1805.
36 DW to RW 23.6.1801.
37 DW to Lady Beaumont 20.4.1806.
38 DW to JM 19.3.1797.
39 DW to JM 19.3.1797.
40 DW to JM 7.3.1796.
41 DW to Mrs. Clarkson 17.7.1803.
42 Table talk of Samuel Rogers, ed. Dyce 1887.
43 Edward Ferguson to Samuel Ferguson 22.7.1805.
44 DW to C. Clarkson 2.3.1806.
45 DW to C. Clarkson 6.6.1808.

A Select Bibliography

Biographical
Dorothy Wordsworth: *The Grasmere Journals* ed. Pamela Woof. (Oxford 1991).
The Letters of William and Dorothy Wordsworth: The Early Years 1787-1805, ed. E. de Selincourt, revised C. L. Shaver 1967).
The Middle Years 1806-1811, ed. E. de Selincourt, revised Mary Moorman (Oxford 1969).
E. de Selincourt, *Dorothy Wordsworth* (Oxford 1933).
Dorothy Wordsworth, *Recollections of a Tour made in Scotland in 1803* (1894).
The Wordsworth Gallery: *Wordsworth & Coleridge at Gallow Hill.*
Eleanor F. Rawnsley, *Grasmere in Wordsworth's Time* (Kendal n.d.).
William Angus Knight, *Dove Cottage, Grasmere* (1900).
B. Kirby, *Lakeland Words* (Batley 1898).
Thomas De Quincey, *Recollections of the Lakes and the Lake Poets* (1970 edn.).
The Golden Age of Travel, ed. Helen Barber Morrison (1953).
William Rollinson, *Life and Tradition in the Lake District* (Clapham 1981).
Mistress Margaret Dods, *Cook and Housewife's Manual* (Edinburgh 1829).

Medical
The London Dispensatory (1814).
G. W. Francis, F. L. S., *The Dictionary of Practical Receipts* (1853).